BRAIN GAMES®
STICKER BY NUMBER™
VINTAGE
BIRDS

How to Sticker by Number™

Find the coordinating stickers in the back of the book to complete the picture. Place the sticker with the same code onto the matching space on the art page. Use the answer key to see the completed pages.

Louis Weber, CEO
Publications International, Ltd.
8140 Lehigh Ave
Morton Grove, IL 60053

Images from Shutterstock.com and rawpixel.com

Permission is never granted for commercial purposes.

ISBN: 978-1-63938-420-4

Manufactured in China.

8 7 6 5 4 3 2 1

Let's get social!
@Publications_International
@PublicationsInternational
@BrainGames.TM
www.pilbooks.com

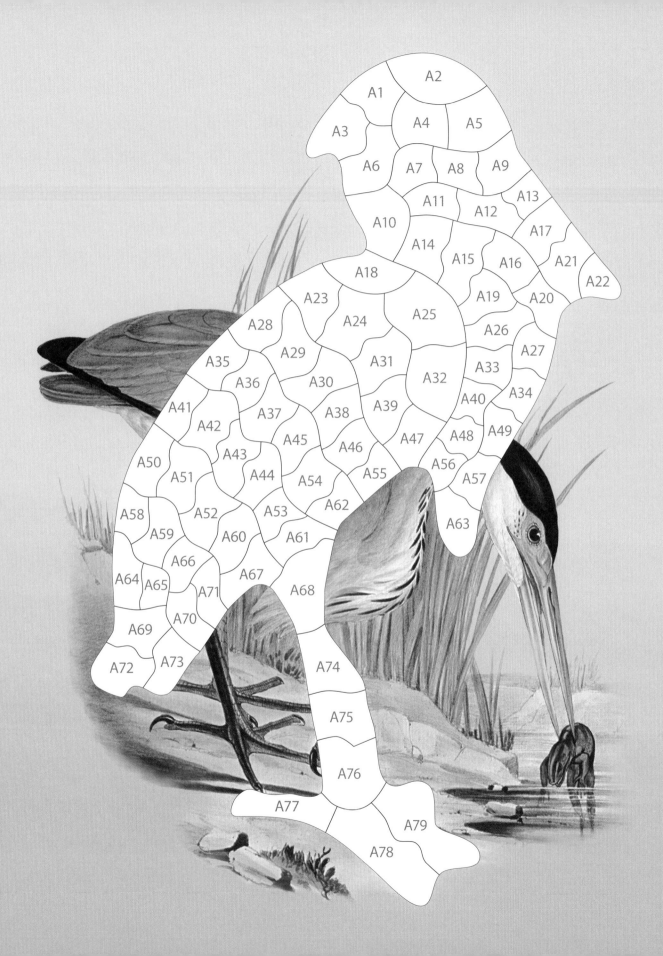

1

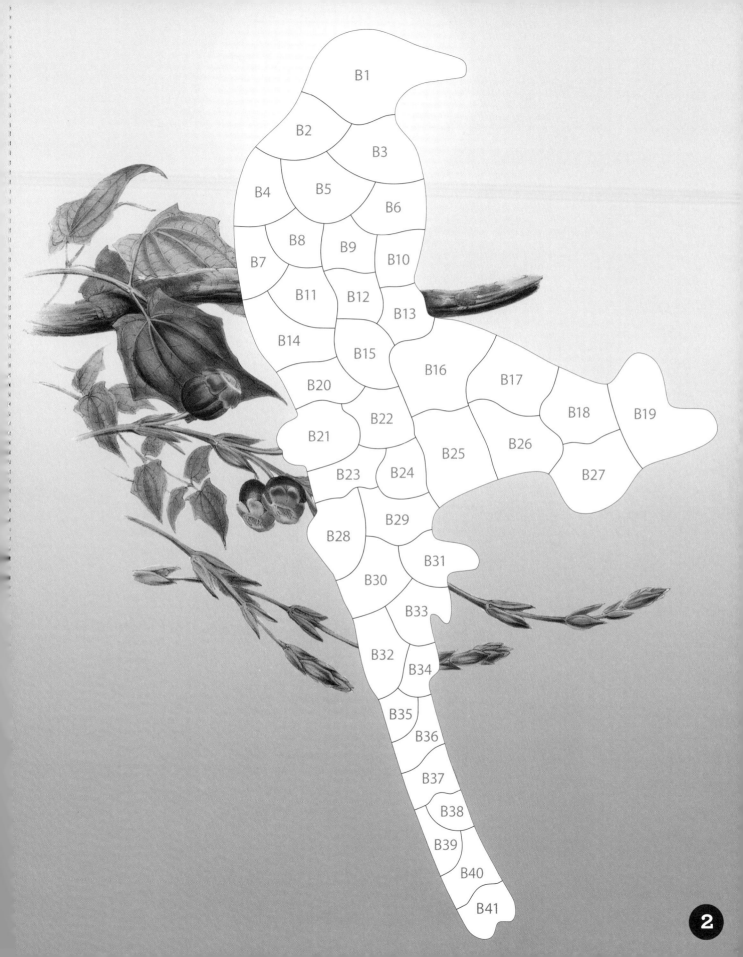

2

3

4

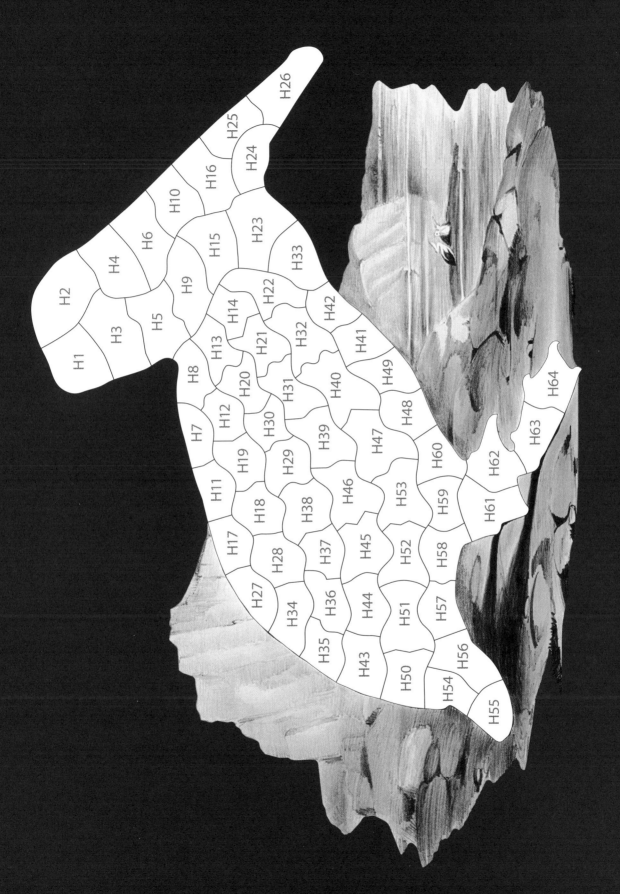

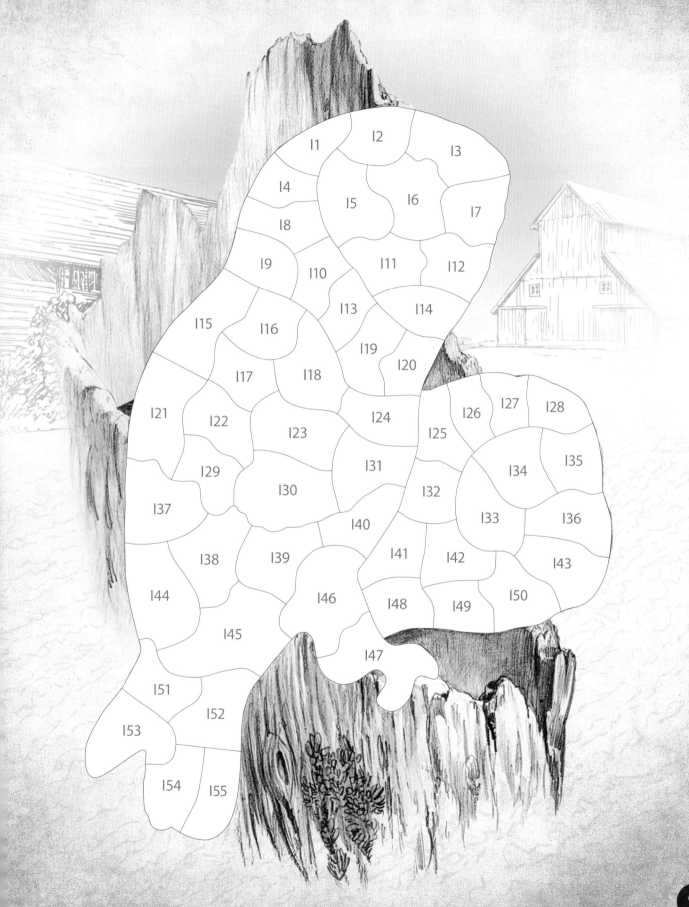

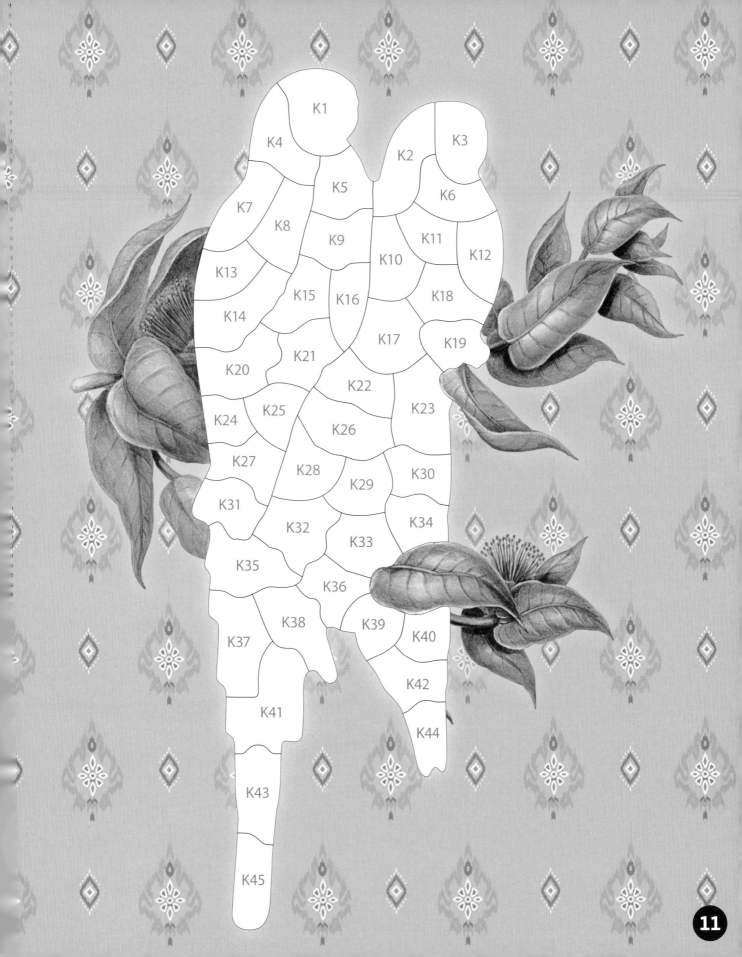

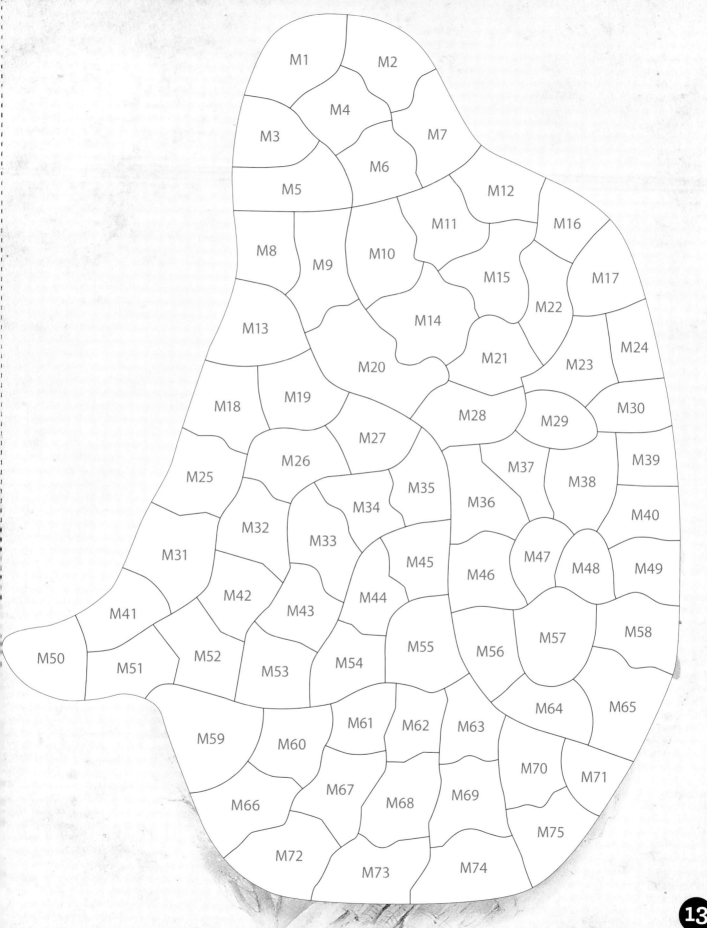

13

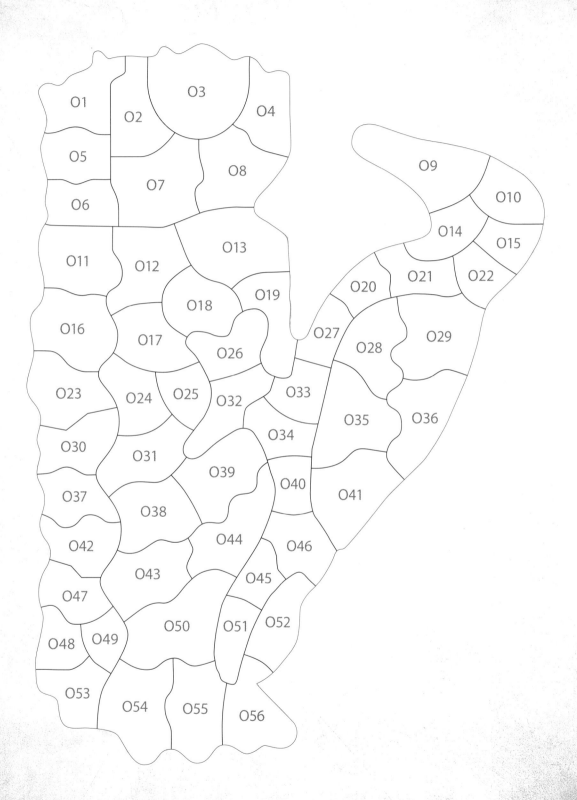

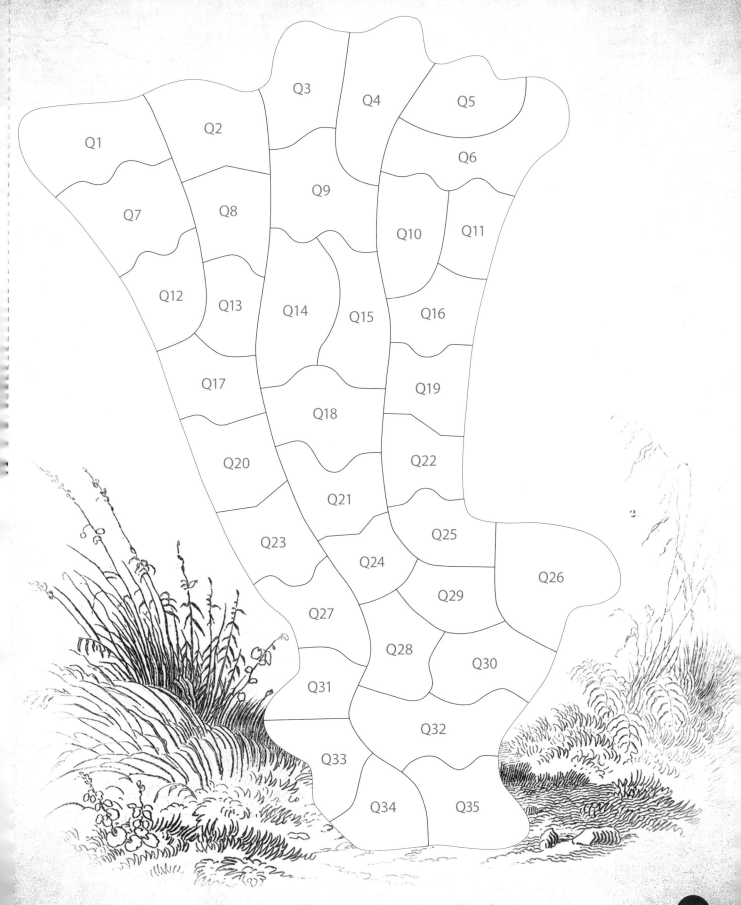

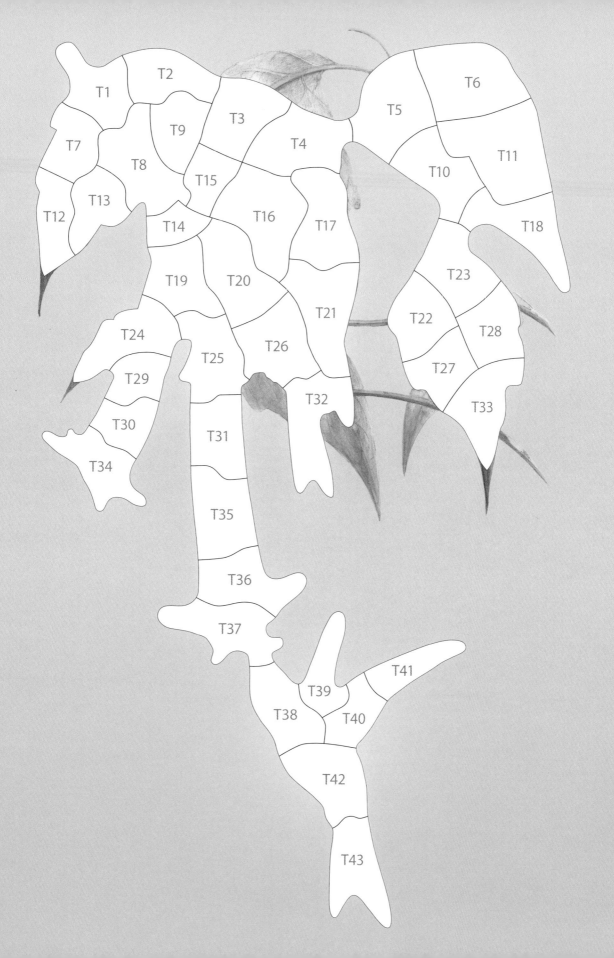

20

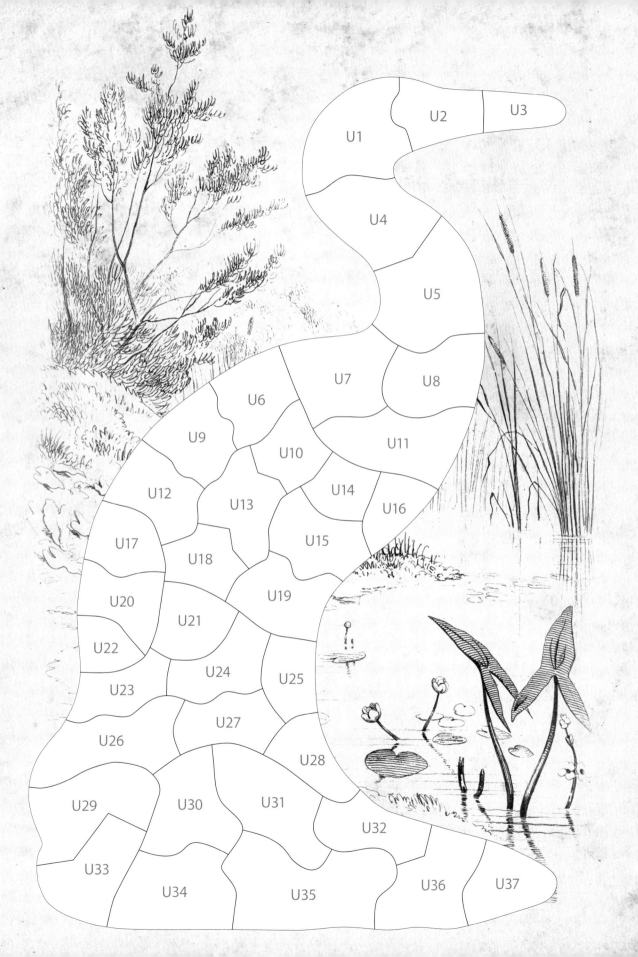

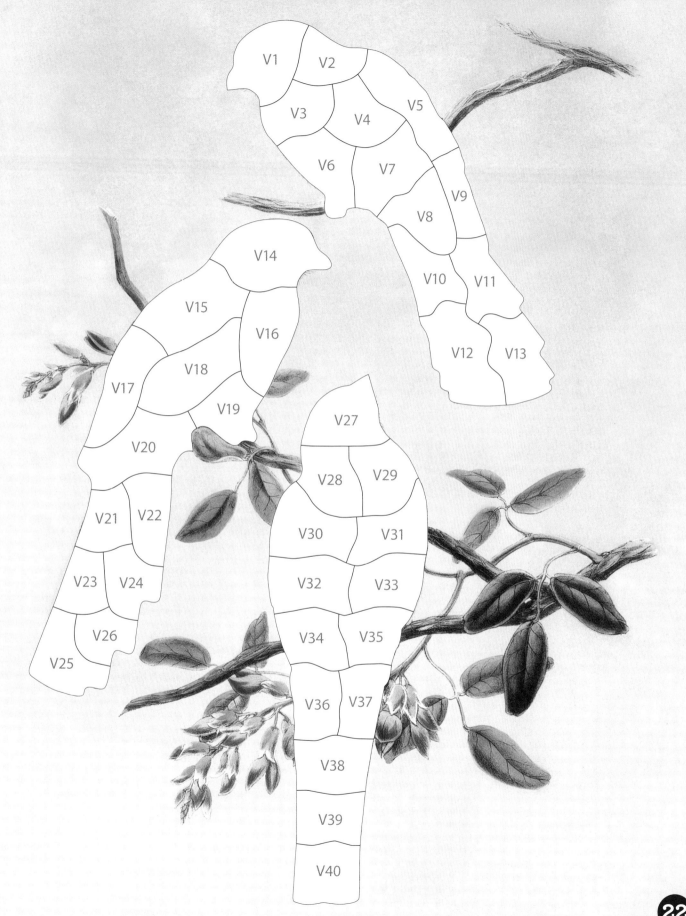

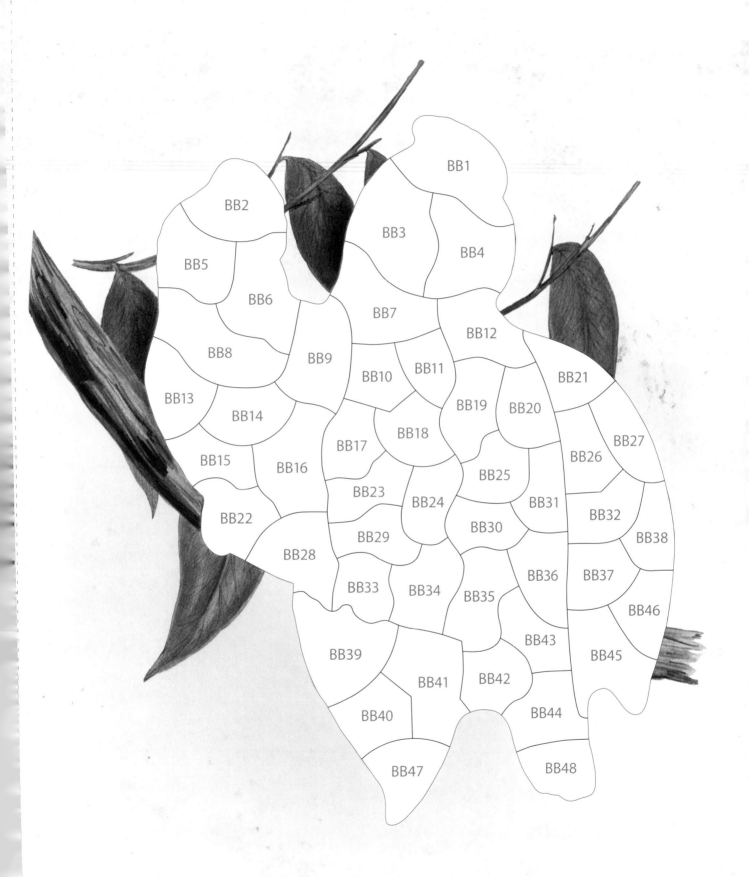

28

9

10

11

12

13

14

15

16

17

18

19

20

21

22

23

24

25

26

27

28

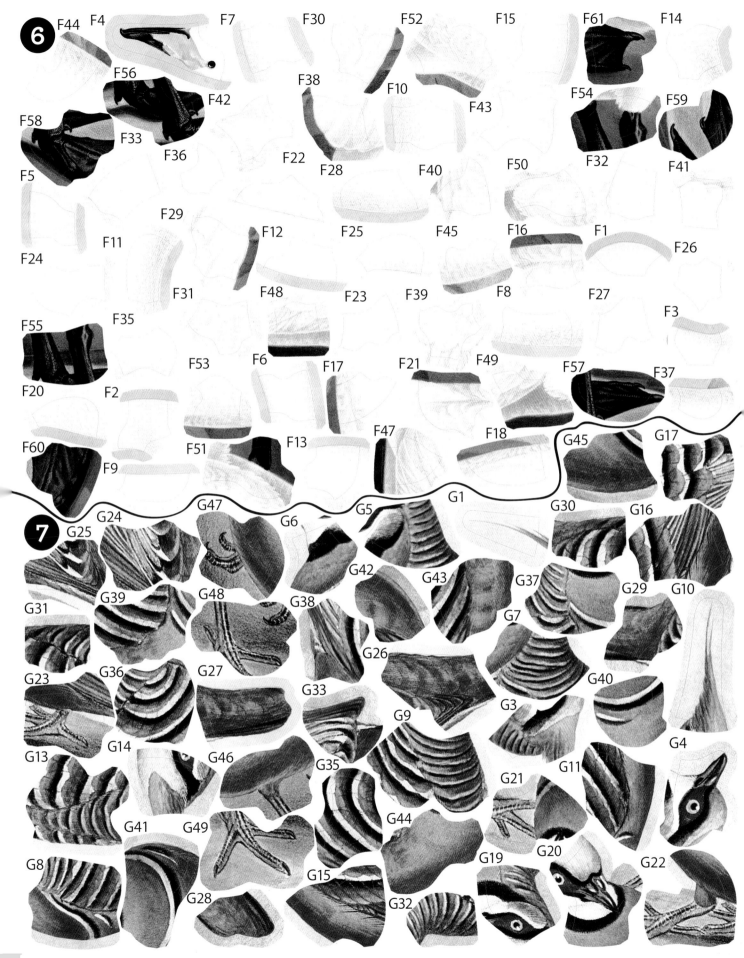

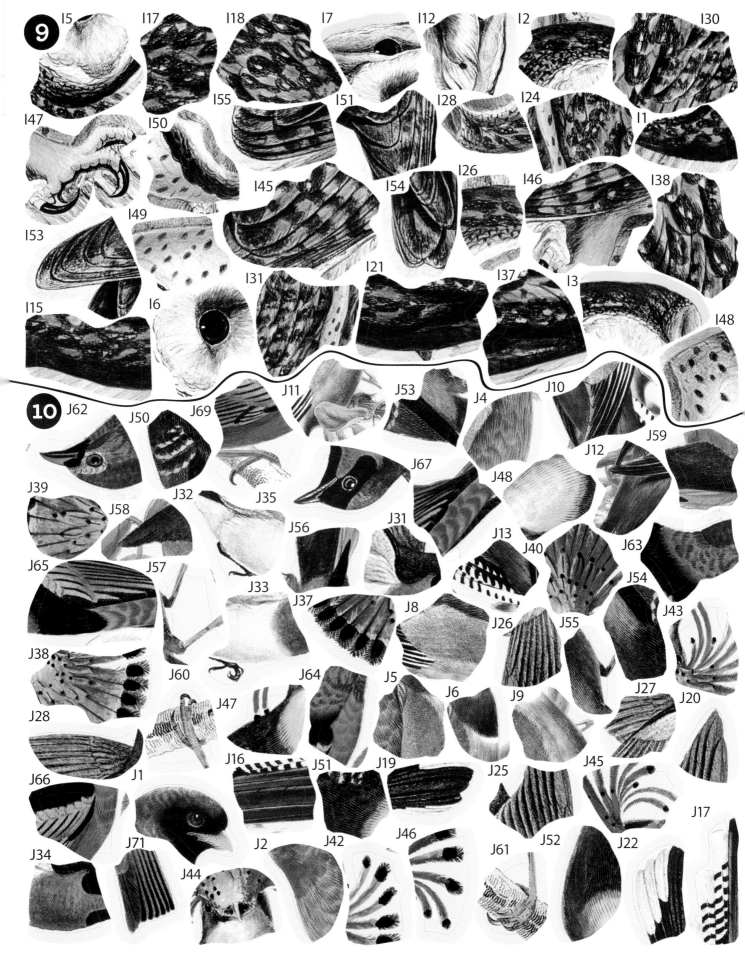

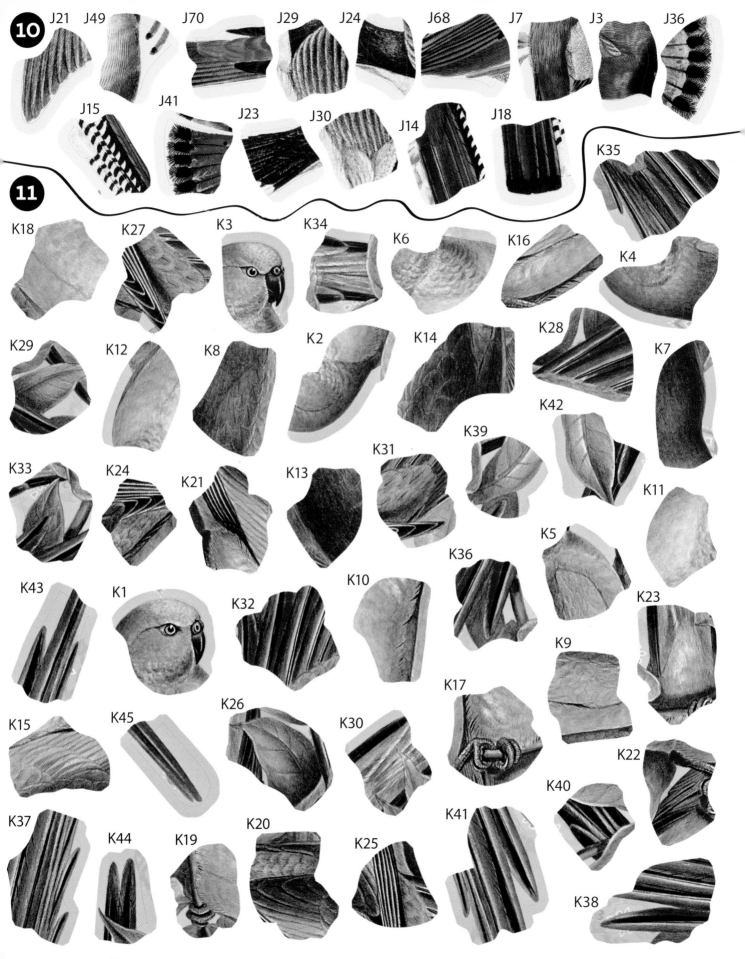

10

J21 J49 J70 J29 J24 J68 J7 J3 J36

J15 J41 J23 J30 J14 J18 K35

11

K18 K27 K3 K34 K6 K16 K4

K29 K12 K8 K2 K14 K28 K7

K42

K33 K24 K21 K13 K31 K39 K11

K5

K43 K1 K32 K10 K36 K23

K9

K17

K15 K45 K26 K30 K22

K40

K37 K44 K19 K20 K25 K41

K38

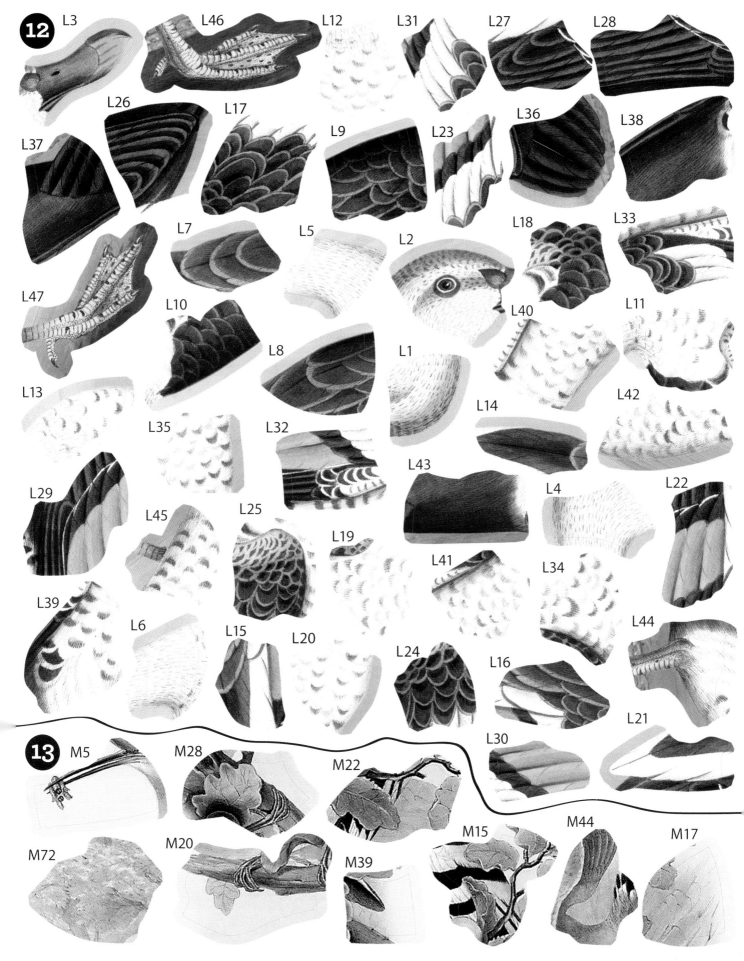

12
L3 L46 L12 L31 L27 L28
L26 L17 L9 L23 L36 L38
L37 L18 L33
L7 L5 L2 L40 L11
L47 L10 L8 L1 L42
L13 L14
L35 L32 L43 L4 L22
L29 L45 L25 L19 L41 L34
L39 L6 L15 L20 L24 L16 L44
L30 L21

13 M5 M28 M22 M44 M17
M72 M20 M39 M15

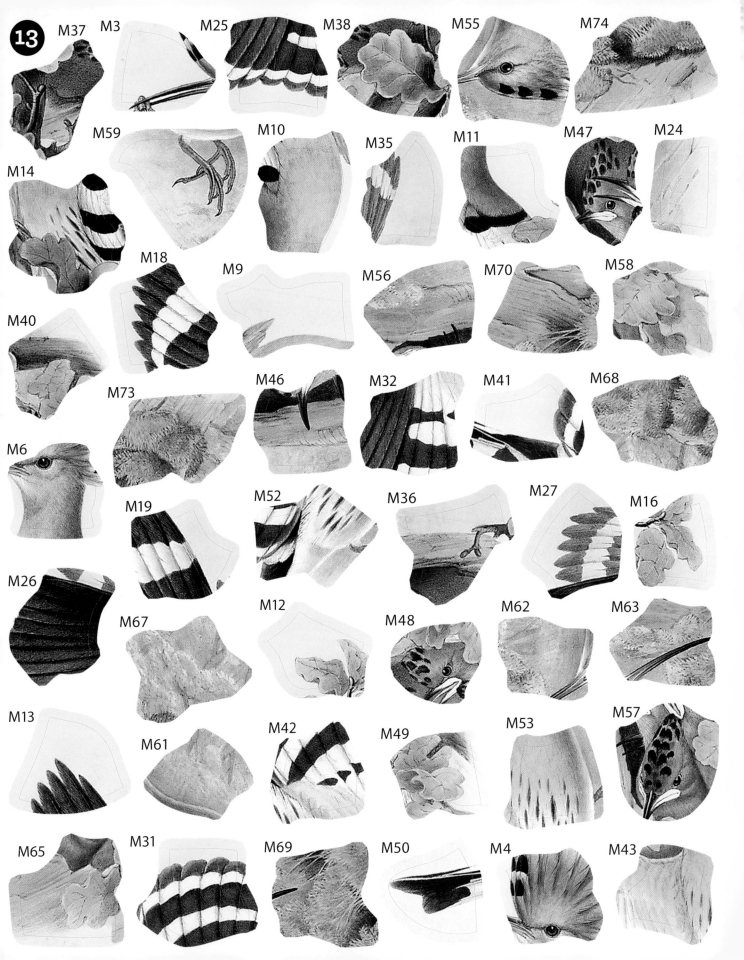

13

M37 M3 M25 M38 M55 M74 M59 M10 M35 M11 M47 M24 M14 M18 M9 M56 M70 M58 M40 M73 M46 M32 M41 M68 M6 M19 M52 M36 M27 M16 M26 M67 M12 M48 M62 M63 M13 M61 M42 M49 M53 M57 M65 M31 M69 M50 M4 M43

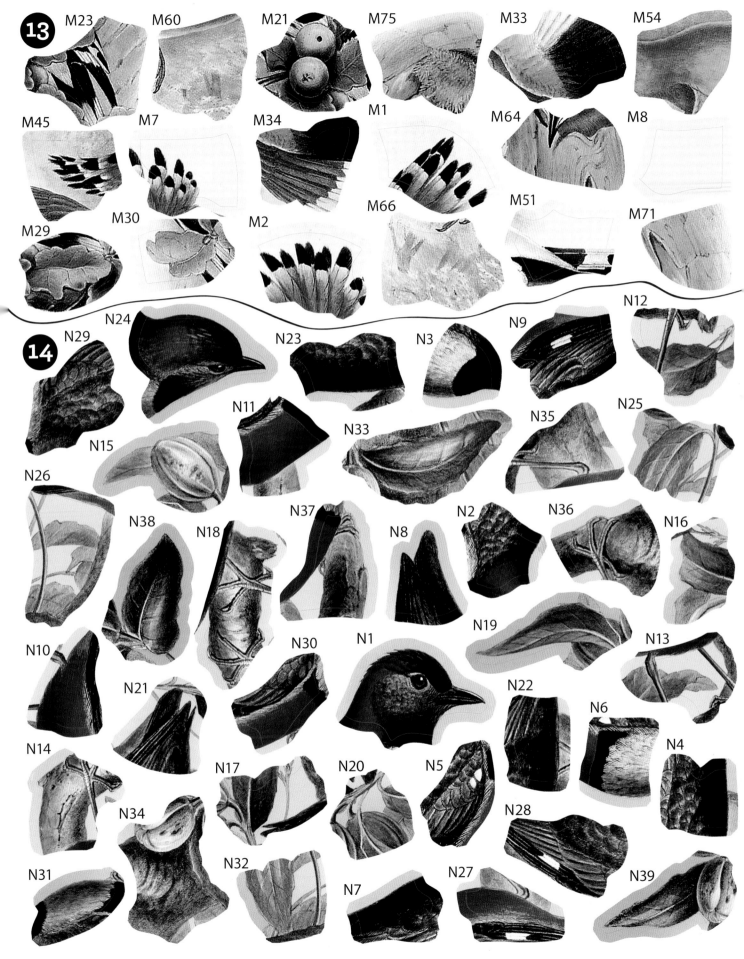

13
M23 M60 M21 M75 M33 M54
M45 M7 M34 M1 M64 M8
M29 M30 M2 M66 M51 M71

14
N29 N24 N23 N3 N9 N12
N11 N33 N35 N25
N26 N15
N38 N18 N37 N8 N2 N36 N16
N10 N19 N13
N21 N30 N1 N22 N6 N4
N14 N17 N20 N5 N28
N34
N31 N32 N7 N27 N39

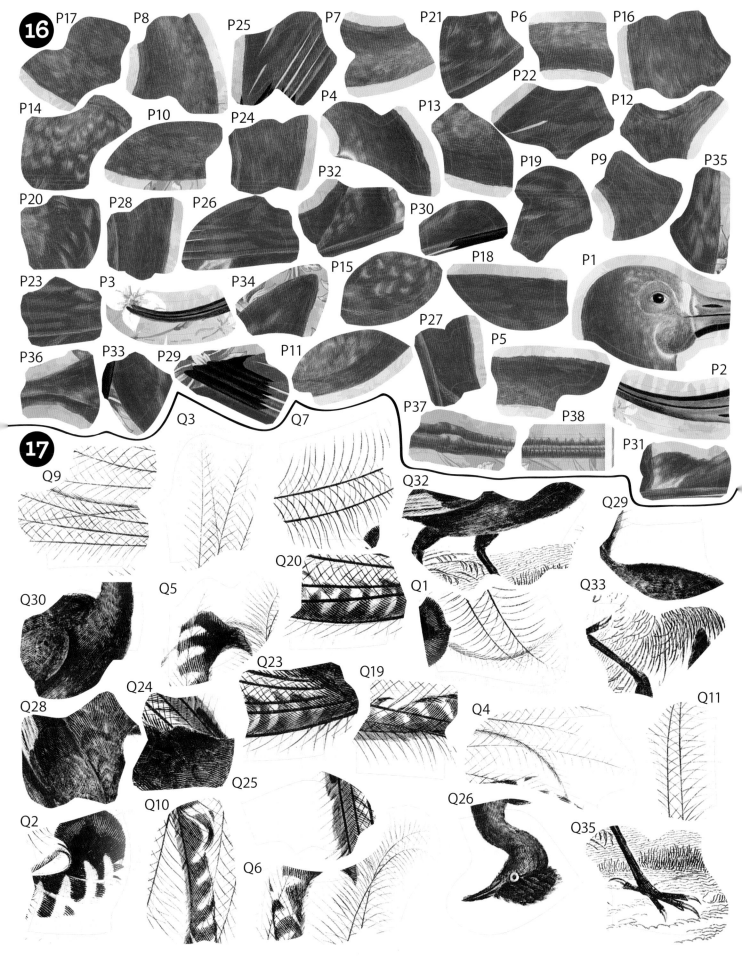

16

P17 P8 P25 P7 P21 P6 P16
P14 P10 P24 P4 P13 P22 P12
P20 P28 P26 P32 P13 P19 P9 P35
P23 P3 P34 P15 P30 P18 P1
P36 P33 P29 P11 P27 P5 P2
P37 P38 P31
Q3 Q7

17

Q9 Q32 Q29
Q30 Q5 Q20 Q1 Q33
Q28 Q24 Q23 Q19 Q4 Q11
Q2 Q10 Q25 Q6 Q26 Q35

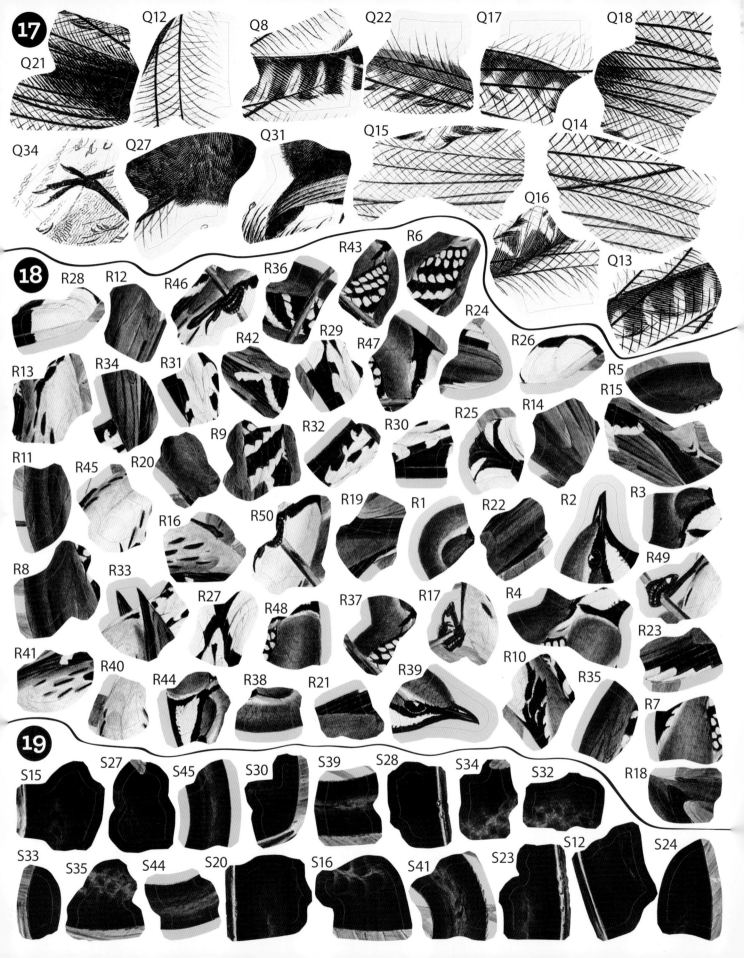

17

Q21   Q12   Q8   Q22   Q17   Q18

Q34   Q27   Q31   Q15   Q14

Q16   Q13

18

R28   R12   R46   R36   R43   R6

R42   R29   R47   R24   R26   R5

R13   R34   R31   R15

R11   R45   R20   R9   R32   R30   R25   R14

R16   R50   R19   R1   R22   R2   R3

R8   R33   R27   R48   R37   R17   R4   R49

R41   R40   R44   R38   R21   R39   R10   R35   R23

R7

19

S15   S27   S45   S30   S39   S28   S34   S32   R18

S33   S35   S44   S20   S16   S41   S23   S12   S24

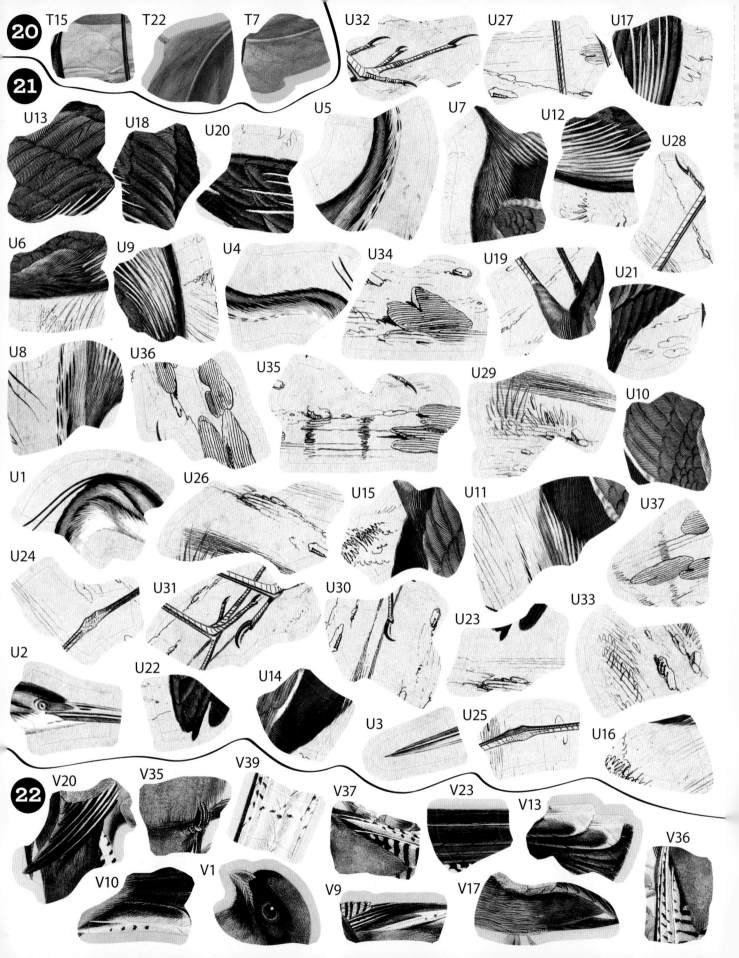

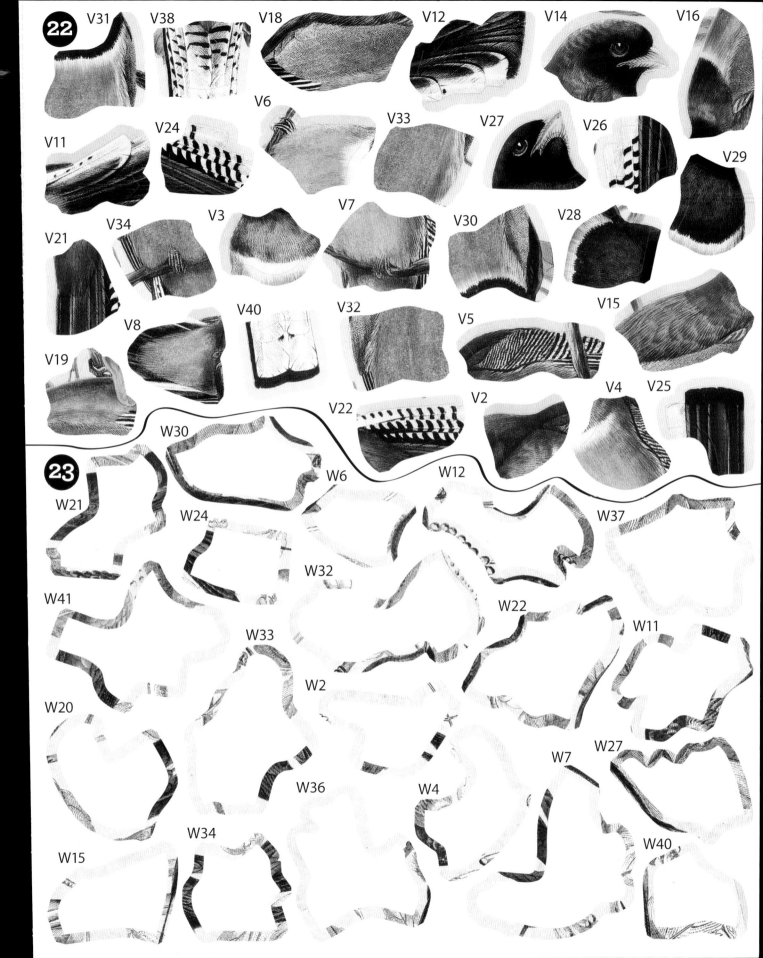

22

V31 V38 V18 V12 V14 V16

V11 V24 V6 V33 V27 V26 V29

V21 V34 V3 V7 V30 V28 V15

V19 V8 V40 V32 V5 V4 V25

V22 V2

23

W30 W6 W12

W21 W24 W37

W41 W32 W22 W11

W20 W33 W2 W27 W7

W36 W4 W40

W15 W34

23

W28 W8 W18 W35 W16

W23 W29 W31 W25

W42 W14

W13 W17

W3 W38 W1

W10 W39 W19

W9 W5

W26

X17 X22 X7

X12

24

X8 X16 X20

X4 X23 X13

X18 X10 X27

X28 X32 X1 X24

X29 X15

X26 X3

X30 X5 X6

X19 X9 X21

X2 X14 X25 X11

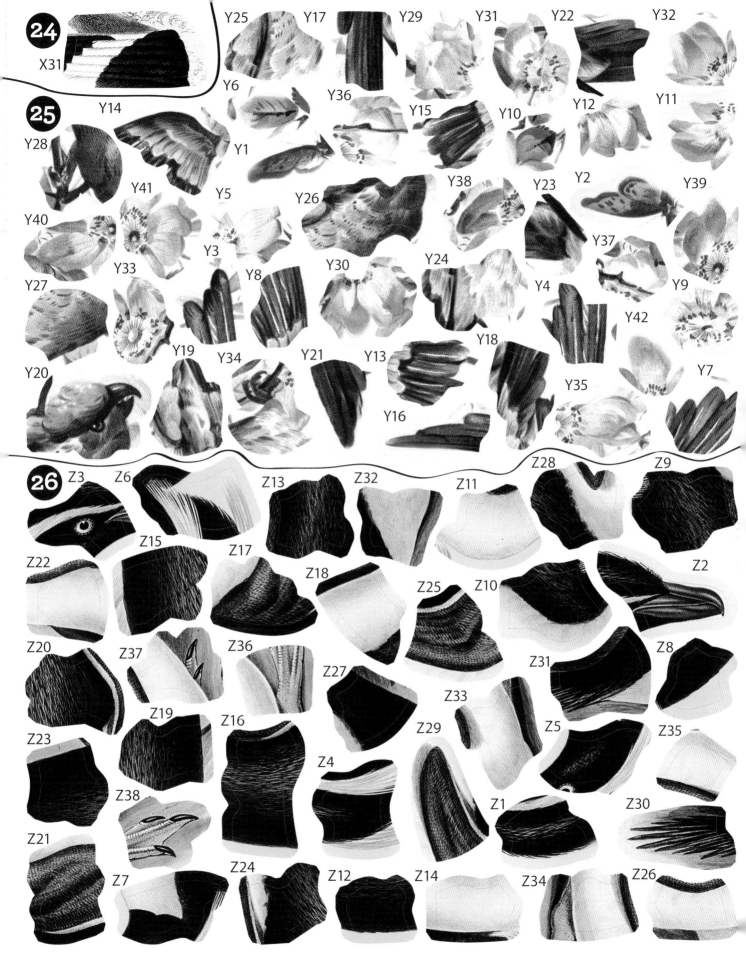

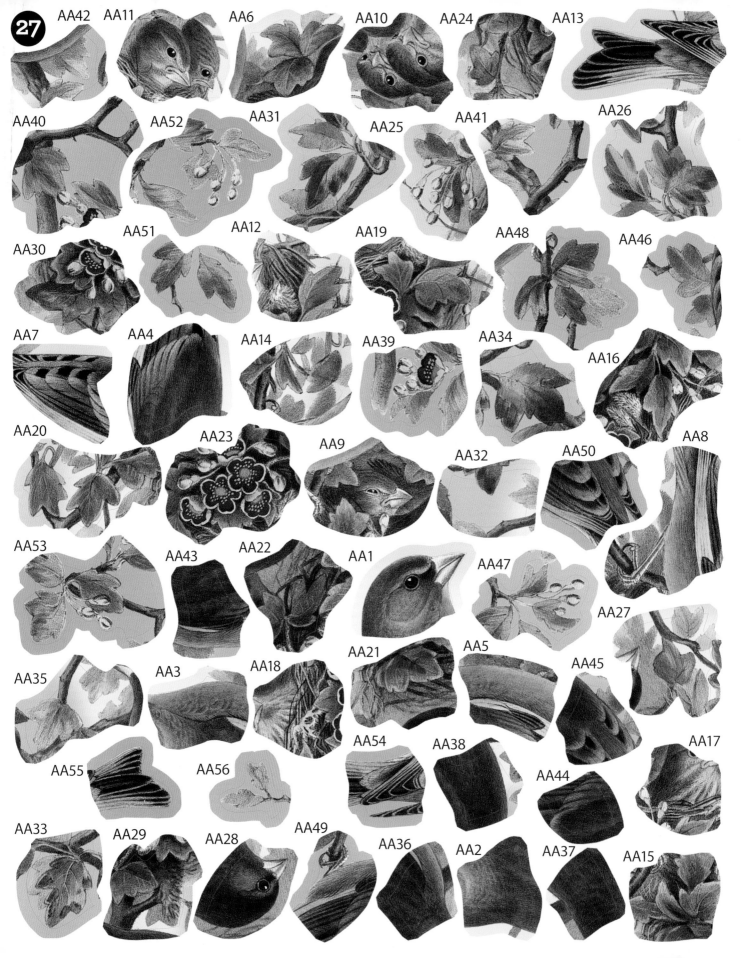

27

AA42 AA11 AA6 AA10 AA24 AA13
AA40 AA52 AA31 AA25 AA41 AA26
AA30 AA51 AA12 AA19 AA48 AA46
AA7 AA4 AA14 AA39 AA34 AA16
AA20 AA23 AA9 AA32 AA50 AA8
AA53 AA43 AA22 AA1 AA47 AA27
AA35 AA3 AA18 AA21 AA5 AA45 AA17
AA55 AA56 AA54 AA38 AA44
AA33 AA29 AA28 AA49 AA36 AA2 AA37 AA15

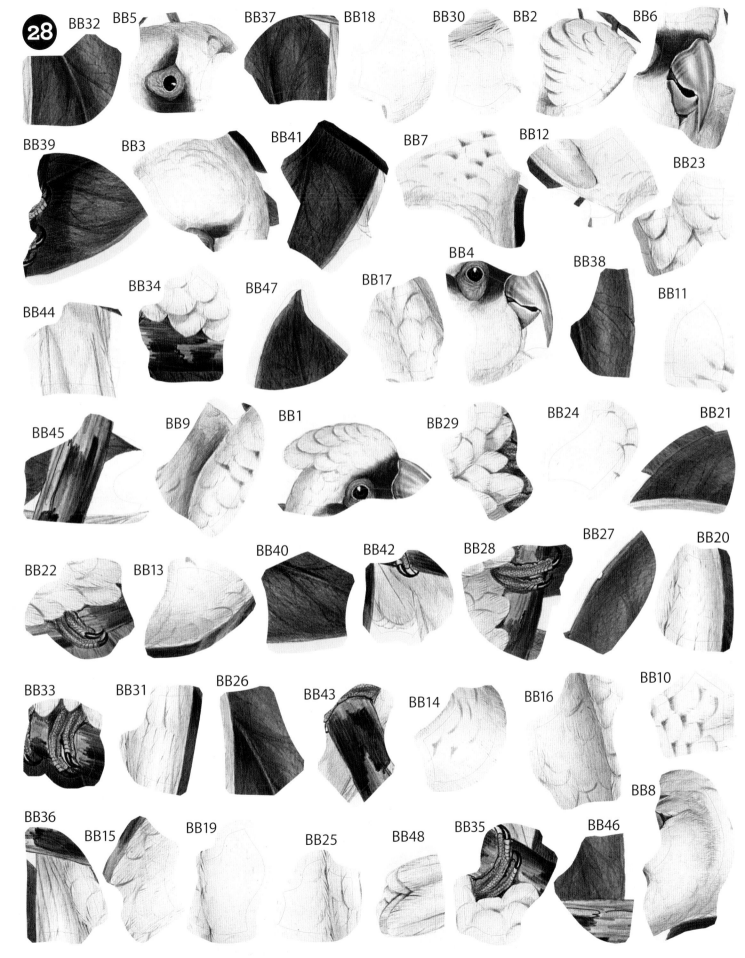

28

BB32 BB5 BB37 BB18 BB30 BB2 BB6

BB39 BB3 BB41 BB7 BB12 BB23

BB44 BB34 BB47 BB17 BB4 BB38 BB11

BB45 BB9 BB1 BB29 BB24 BB21

BB22 BB13 BB40 BB42 BB28 BB27 BB20

BB33 BB31 BB26 BB43 BB14 BB16 BB10

BB8

BB36 BB15 BB19 BB25 BB48 BB35 BB46